The Unwavering Faith

Rev. Harris D. McFarlane

The Unwavering Faith

Copyright © 2022 by **Rev. Harris D. McFarlane**

Paperback ISBN: 978-1-952098-97-0

eBook ISBN: 978-1-957809-10-6

Printed in the United States of America. All rights reserved solely by the author. No part of this book may be reproduced in any form or by any means, without the written permission of the author.

Unless otherwise indicated, Bible quotations are taken from the Holy Bible, King James Version®. Copyright © 1982 by Thomas Nelson, Inc. Used by permission.

Published By Cornerstone Publishing

info@thecornerstonepublishers.com

www.thecornerstonepublishers.com

CONTACT INFORMATION

To order bulk copies of this book, please send email to:

info@dimensionministries.org

Contents

Introduction 5
1. The Ultimate Power 9
2. Engage The Law of Belief 21
3. The Law of Expectation 29
4. Discipline Your Expectations 39
5. Dare To Dream 49
6. Speaking Words of Power 57
7. The Place of Prayer 65
8. Step Out and Win 75
9. Unwavering Faith 83
10. Choose Faith Over Fear 93
11. About the Author 101

Introduction

Unwavering faith in God is an omnipotent power capable of unlocking a world of endless possibilities. For only on the rock of faith can anything lasting be established. Faith is accepting and believing as true that which our senses defy. Faith is trusting God to turn dreams into reality. "Faith is the substance of things hoped for; the evidence of things not seen." (Hebrew 11:1(KJV)). It is like the seeds you deposit in the ground; you cannot see them, but when you nurture, water, fertilize, and nourish them, they accelerate and grow after their kind. Faith believes in what you can't see with your natural eyes. You can undoubtedly accomplish what you can conceive and believe through the power of unwavering faith in God. Jesus said it this way: "... if thou canst believe, all things are possible to him that believeth." (Mark 9:23 (KJV))

"For what is faith unless it is to believe in what you do not see."

-St.Augustine

Nothing in this world will take the place of faith, and nothing can suffice for lack of it. Education cannot, position will not, and intellectual prowess will not. Not even hope can. Life will bless you according to your level of faith and curse you based on your unbelief. Faith will keep you afloat despite any flood or challenge that life may bring. It is the game-changer in the journey of life. Whenever things are tough, and you want to have a beautiful experience, all you need to do is connect with God, trust Him, and maintain unwavering faith, belief, and expectancy. Once you do that, you automatically open up a channel for the miraculous power of the almighty God. Things will work so well for you that you won't even realize how tough things are. "For verily I say unto you, If ye have faith as a grain of mustard seed, ye shall say unto the mountain, Remove hence to yonder place, and it shall remove, and nothing shall be impossible unto you." (Matthew 17:20 (KJV))

"Blessed is the man that trusteth in the LORD, and whose hope the LORD is. For he shall be as a tree planted by the waters, and that spreadeth out her roots by the river, and shall not see when heat cometh, but her leaf shall be green; and shall not be careful in the year of drought, neither shall cease from yielding fruit." (Jeremiah 17:7-8 (KJV))

Faith is not a feeling; it is an internal conviction that compels you to act on the word of God. Faith, therefore, would persist even in times of difficulty when everything seems to contradict your belief. I am talking about times when you don't feel like going on. Faith will move you to take steps forward regardless of how you feel. Life is full of challenges and situations capable of driving someone crazy.

But that is why you need a different perspective on life; believe me, perspective is everything. How you see life or a situation is how you will live or respond to that situation. The way you view tomorrow is the way you will experience it. In other words, perspective is very vital in our lives. Yes, things may not have turned out the way you planned, but you have to understand that God has a bigger and better plan in store for you. It all depends on your perspective. Therefore, you have to focus on the positive side of things rather than the negative ones, which lead to doom. And like Wayne Dyer said, "If you believe it'll work out, you'll see opportunities. If you don't believe it'll work out, you'll see obstacles. Now, it's up to you."

When the tide changes against you and the floods of negativity seem to close in on your dreams, faith is your best bait to stay afloat. And in the wake of the current global challenges, as occasioned by the recent pandemic and the Ukraine war, with men's hearts begging to fail them by the day, there is no better time to unleash your faith than now. That is the essence of this book. If you can unlock your faith and get rid of fear, doubt, and unbelief, you will enjoy the consistent victory, but you will practically soar into new levels of accomplishment in life. I sincerely hope that as you read, you will gain deep insights that will position you at the topmost top in life. Cheers!

CHAPTER ONE

The Ultimate Power

There is no power greater than the power of faith. It is the PowerPoint of destiny and the passcode that unlocks all of the abilities and resources of God. Faith will open the door to success, advancement, influence, protection, healing, and prosperity. That is what connects your natural efforts with the supernatural power of God, giving you an extraordinary advantage over all of life's circumstances.

Faith transports your dreams and aspirations from the invisible realm into the visible realm, where you can practically live them. Faith is the ultimate power—available for the recovery and the preservation of human destinies. It is the timeless weapon for gaining complete victory overall life's challenges. With faith in place, you can glide effortlessly through the high places of life.

Nothing in this world will take the place of faith, and nothing can suffice for lack of it. Education cannot, connections cannot, position will not, intellectual prowess will not, and even hope will not; indeed, unwavering faith in God is an omnipotent power. Life will bless you according to your level of faith and curse you based on your unbelief. Faith will keep you afloat despite any flood or challenge that life may bring. It is the game-changer in the journey of life.

Your faith commits God's abilities and resources to you. It also put His integrity on the line. This is one of the primary reasons God cannot fail to fulfill His promise to us. That is what makes faith possible in the first place.

God cannot only do whatever He promised in His word, but he is also faithful enough to do what He promised. How do you live a life of faith? Live by the promises of God. When you live a life based on God's promises, you live a powerful life. Believe solely in the promises of God. What is a promise? "An offer with a guaranteed result." This is so powerful. The promises of God will never let you down. Human beings often break promises. But the promises of God will never fail. It is done to you as you believe. In other words, it is done according to the measure of your faith.

If You Can Believe

If you can believe and act accordingly, nothing can be impossible for you. "Jesus said unto him if thou canst believe, all things are possible to him that believeth." (Mark 9:23 (KJV)). Your poverty can be turned into riches, your weaknesses can be turned into strength, and your adversity can become your greatest opportunity. Your dreams can become your reality if you can believe.

If you have faith, you have God on your side and, therefore, the full power and resources of His at your disposal. It doesn't matter what is against you; either way, you win when God is on your side! Remember, one with God is always the majority.

How Faith Works

To operate in faith, you have to have a deep-seated understanding of how faith works: The question is, how does faith work in our lives? How can one freely operate in faith?

First, faith comes from the revelation of the word of God, which begins with hearing the word of God. "So, then faith cometh by hearing, and hearing by the word of God." (Romans 10:17 (KJV)).

In other words, God is not responsible for your having or not having faith; you are. And the reason is simple; He has already revealed how faith comes to us. So, whether you have faith or not is entirely up to you. But once you receive faith-filled words into your heart, faith will erupt on your inside.

Faith is birthed in your heart every time you are truly exposed to God's revelation of knowledge.

Mary Heard the Word

Now, see what happened to Mary the day the Angel, Gabriel, brought her a word from the Lord:

"And the angel came in unto her, and said, Hail, thou that art highly favored, the Lord is with thee: blessed art thou among women. And when she saw him, she was troubled at his saying and cast in her mind what manner of salutation this should be. And the angel said unto her, Fear not, Mary: for thou hast found favor with God. And, behold, thou shalt conceive in thy womb and bring forth a son, and shalt call his name Jesus. He shall be great, and shall be called the Son of the Highest: and the Lord God shall give unto him the throne of his father David: And he shall reign over the house of Jacob forever, and of his kingdom, there shall be no end." (Luke 1:28-33 (KJV))

She Believed the Word

When Mary heard those words from the angel and believed them, faith was born. Of course, she wanted to know how those things would come to pass, considering that she had not known any man. She asked the angel a question:

"Then said Mary unto the angel, How shall this be, seeing I know not a man? And the angel answered and said unto her, The Holy Ghost shall come upon thee, and the power of the Highest shall overshadow thee: therefore, also that holy thing which shall be born of thee shall be called the Son of God. And, behold, thy cousin Elisabeth, she hath also conceived a son in her old age: and this is the sixth month with her, who was called barren. For with God, nothing shall be impossible." (Luke 1:34-37 (KJV))

Mary was confused by the angel's words and wondered what they meant, and also because she didn't know who she was and who God was. Yet as soon as she was convinced about those words, she believed. The phrase "you are truly blessed" was used in those days to address and honor a unique group of people, such as kings, priests, prophets, and dignitaries like the popes. So, when Mary heard that salutation from the angel, "Hail, favored one," it didn't fit her personality. She was only a teenager. But when the word came, Mary believed! She practically went from confusion to commitment when she received the Word.

She Confessed the Word

But then, she did something else; she expressed her faith in the words she had received. In other words, she released her faith through the spoken word. The first step to faith is hearing the word and believing it in your heart.

Once you receive a word in your heart and believe it, start confessing your faith; declare God's word (or the specific word spoken to you) regarding that situation. What you decree in words will undoubtedly come to fruition.

"And Mary said, Behold the handmaid of the Lord; be it unto me according to thy word. And the angel departed from her." (Luke 1:38 (KJV))

Mary simply released her faith through words. And I dare say that if you truly believe, you will speak. We will deal with this a little more in another chapter. After that comes the action part of faith. Mary acted on the word of God.

"And Mary arose in those days, and went into the hill country with haste, into a city of Juda; And entered into the house of Zacharias, and saluted Elisabeth." (Luke 1:39-40 (KJV))

So, first, you need to hear the word, believe, confess, and act on what you believe. Remember, your actions are the most authentic proof of your faith. It is your action that brings your faith expectation into manifestation. In essence, it is an action that translates your desires into reality. Faith will erupt in your life if you hear, believe, and act on God's word!

Where Faith Leads

Claiming to have faith without taking the proper steps is an illusion. However, acting on your faith will cost you something. In other words, sometimes faith will lead you to the most uncomfortable circumstances before they eventually produce the desired results.

That was precisely the case with Moses; his faith led him to the place of risk. There was a significant risk for every step he took to accomplish all of the feats he is known for today. For instance, the crossing of the Red Sea was a dangerous adventure. We know it was a risk because those Egyptians who followed them into the sea drowned. I mean, every one of them.

"...By faith they passed through the Red Sea as by dry land: which the Egyptians assaying to do were drowned." (Hebrews 11:29 (KJV))

Can you imagine what it must have been like to lift a simple rod and have a sea of that magnitude divide before you; and convince over three million people, including women and children, to join you in the sea? What if the wall of water collapses back into its original position? What if Pharaoh and his men caught up with them? Or what if the water did not respond so quickly to the drowned Pharaoh's soldiers who were right behind them? Moses courageously led the people in and out of the Red Sea; there are just so many unanswered questions and many things that could have gone wrong.

But that is just the nature of faith; it is risky.

It was risky for Peter to step out of the boat and walk on water. Of course, it was comfortable in the boat, but because he wanted to experience a new dimension in God, he was willing to take the risk. (Matthew 14:28-29 (KJV)).

It was risky for the woman with the issue of blood to break a long-standing Jewish law, press through the crowd, and touch the hem of Jesus' garment, despite hemorrhaging (Matthew 9:20-22 (KJV)). That was very risky because she could have easily been stoned to death if only they had known she was hemorrhaging. Faith is a venture with many risks. However, you cannot reap the benefits of such risks if you do not take them. You will not see the manifestations of many things you desire; they will be dead dreams. I pray for you that your dream will not die!

Four Choices to the Blessing

For you to experience the blessings of God in your life, here are the four things you must do:

1. You must let go of doubt.

If you want to connect with the higher workings of God, you must choose to live and walk by faith. You must choose faith instead of doubt. The Bible says that every believer must live by faith.

"Now the just shall live by faith: but if any man draws back, my soul shall have no pleasure in him." (Hebrew 10:38 (KJV))

Faith is a choice, just as doubt is a choice. You either choose to trust God or doubt Him. And one beautiful thing about every choice we make in life is that they all have positive or negative consequences. Every choice you make either triggers a blessing or a curse. If you doubt God, you short-circuit yourself from His workings. You cannot doubt Him and expect to receive answers from Him.

"But let him ask in faith, nothing wavering. For he that wavereth is like a wave of the sea driven with the wind and tossed. For let, not that man think that he shall receive anything of the Lord." (James 1:6-7 (KJV))

"Yes, be bold and strong! Banish doubt out of your life, realizing that "...the Lord your God is with you wherever you go." (Joshua 1:9 (LB))

2. Look for a promise.

For faith is what defines what a believer should or should not expect from God. We don't just come to Him because we have needs; we come to Him based on His word. So, if you locate a promise like Joshua, you will have a better footing to make your claims and have them taken care of. God's promise to Joshua was to possess every place they trod upon.

"Every place that the sole of your foot shall tread upon, that have I given unto you, as I said unto Moses." (Joshua 1:3 (KJV))

And that became the basis of his claims from God. And as he stood upon the promises of God to them, God confirmed His word to them throughout the lifetime of Joshua. That was exactly the seat he affirmed at the end of his life.

"And, behold, this day I am going the way of all the earth: and ye know in all your hearts and in all your souls, that not one thing hath failed of all the good things which the LORD your God spake concerning you; all are come to pass unto you, and not one thing hath failed thereof." (Joshua 23:14 (KJV))

3. Lean on the Lord.

To enjoy the best of God in life, you have to learn to lean on him; you have to learn to depend on Him for guidance. "In a dream, in a vision of the night, when deep sleep falleth upon men, in slumbering upon the bed; Then he openeth the ears of men, and sealeth their instruction." (Job 33:15-16 (KJV))

"Trust in the LORD with all thine heart, and lean not unto thine own understanding. In all thy ways acknowledge him, and he shall direct thy paths." (Proverbs 3:5-6 (KJV))

4. Launch out in faith.

The next thing you need to do is to launch out in faith. Faith is never passive but an ever-active force that shifts results and commands. When you are truly in the faith zone, you make moves.

"Then Joshua commanded the officers of the people, saying, pass through the host, and command the people, saying, prepare you victuals; for within three days ye shall pass over this Jordan, to go in to possess the land, which the LORD your God giveth you to possess it." (Joshua 1:10-11 (KJV))

"If you wait for perfect conditions, you will never get anything done." If you insist on solving all the problems before you make a decision, you'll never know the thrill of living by faith. God always uses imperfect people in imperfect situations to accomplish his will."(Ecclesiastes 11:4 (LB))

It takes faith both to pursue and fulfill your destiny in God. God has a purpose for your life far above what you can imagine for yourself—a life of meaning, significance, and connection. And it begins with a commitment to believe and act on His word.

You are here to live a full and happy life, glorify God, and enjoy Him indefinitely. All the world's spiritual, mental, and material riches are gifts from God, good in themselves and capable of good use. And as you decide to put your faith in God, not only will you have riches and honor; joy and fulfillment will become your reality. "But as many as received him, to them gave he the power to become the sons of God, even to them that believe on his name." (John 1:12 (KJV))

Chapter Two

Engage the Law of Belief

If you want to operate at a level of life where no obstacle can stop or defeat you, you have to engage the laws of belief. Thinking the right thoughts is a prerequisite to everything. Our ability to originate strong thoughts and mentally move in a thought-filled world is our guarantee of abundant life. This is why a positive belief is a powerful asset in life. Without a positive belief system, you cannot make significant advancements in your life.

A belief is simply a feeling of certainty that someone or something exists or that something is true; a feeling that something is good, right, or valuable; or a feeling of trust in the worth or the ability of someone or something. A belief is also a state or habit in which trust or confidence is placed in some person or thing.

The Power of Belief

There is power in a positive belief. You can turn adverse circumstances to your advantage with a positive belief. It doesn't matter the odds against you; you can change things.

"Therefore, I say unto you, What things soever ye desire

when ye pray, believe that ye receive them, and ye shall have them." (Mark 11:24 (KJV))

"But Jesus beheld them, and said unto them, With men this is impossible, but with God all things are possible." (Matthew 19:26 (KJV))

Remember, belief and purpose in the imagination make the difference in a dreamer's life. Without a positive slant on things, mere dreaming will not amount to much; you have to believe.

"And all things, whatsoever ye shall ask in prayer, believing, ye shall receive…Then touched he their eyes, saying, according to your faith be it unto you." (Matthew 9:29 (KJV))

A positive belief does not necessarily mean denying the fact, but it means holding on to the truth you have, adhering to an inner sense stronger than all the obstacles against you. In other words, while you can't deny the diagnosis, you can defy the doctor's verdict. There is a vast difference between those. If you realize that God is on your side and that His almighty power is available at your disposal, it will completely change your perspective and, by extension, your experiences. The same power that raised Jesus Christ from the dead is available to us. Sadly, because we don't use the power of belief, this extraordinary power of God placed within us eventually eludes us. Sometimes, it becomes dormant and useless. In other words, when we're not connected to the true vine, which is our power source, then the life that flows from Him has no way of getting to us (John 15:1-5 (KJV)). And this means that our light, strength, and power go dim and weak.

But the moment you believe, you automatically connect to God's inexhaustible resource of power and all possibilities. Over two thousand years ago, when Jesus came back to life, everything changed. Without being plugged into the power source, there's no way to fulfill your purpose. An unplugged blender is useless.

If you get connected to this power, you will experience abundance instead of lack. You will experience wisdom instead of superstition; you will experience peace instead of inner strife, joy instead of sadness, light instead of darkness, harmony instead of discord; you will experience faith and confidence instead of fear and worry. The question is, how do you start this incredible journey in your life?

"Therefore, I say unto you, what things soever ye desire when he pray, believe that ye receive them, and he shall have them." (Mark 11:24 (KJV))

The Law of Belief

The law of belief states that whatever you believe with feelings (emotions) becomes your reality. That means that whatever you believe and expect becomes your self-fulfilling prophecy. William Carrie said, "Expect great things from God, and attempt great things for God because that brings honor to Him."

When you understand the law of belief, not only does it liberate you from every shackle of external limitations, it empowers you to determine your outcomes in life. Many people do not realize that they can determine the course of their lives. But with a good grasp of the law of belief, you are well on your way to living life on your terms. If truth be told, you are not supposed to depend on external forces to govern your life. If you do, you will have relinquished responsibility to the wrong forces. Remember, external forces do not work to your advantage unless you intentionally learn to use them for your benefit.

Put Your Mind to Work

Think about the prodigal son if you want to understand how powerful your mind can be. The study of the prodigal son is a classic example of how the life of anyone can be transformed through the power of the mind. It is the story of a young man who had asked his father to give him his portion of the inheritance while the father was still alive.

"And he said, A certain man had two sons: And the younger of them said to his father, Father, give me the portion of goods that falleth to me. And he divided unto them his living. And not many days after, the younger son gathered all together, and took his journey into a far country, and there wasted his substance with riotous living. And when he had spent all, there arose a mighty famine in that land; and he began to be in want. And he went and joined himself to a citizen of that country, and he sent him into his fields to feed swine. And he would fain have filled his belly with the husks that the swine did eat: and no man gave unto him." (Luke 15:11-16(KJV))

The problem was not necessarily because he asked for his inheritance; it was his after all, but the problem was that he collected it, went out there, and wasted the entire fund living a wild life—a lifestyle of luxury and folly. It wasn't long before he squandered the resources and was in a terrible place financially. He went from surplus to scarcity (broke). In fact, at one point, his financial situation was so bad that he couldn't even take care of his basic needs of food, clothes, and shelter. That was how he ended up with pigs. Long story short, after facing humiliation for a while, he sat down to evaluate his life. He decided to engage his mental capacity. While he was thinking deeply, he got an idea about how to liberate himself from hunger, deprivation, and all kinds of things. In the end, he came to a resolution to return and reunite with his father. I love the way the scripture renders it. The King James Version said, "when he came to himself..."

One powerful thing about him was that the moment he discerned what to do through engaging his mind, he got up and took steps. Verse 20 of the same passage of scripture says, "And he arose, and came to his father..." Of course, his father received him with joy and threw a party for him despite his previous wrong decision (verses 22-24). But it was the decision to engage his mind that made the difference. His transformation was only possible simply because he chose to believe in his father's unconditional love.

How to stay confident and anchored with optimism:

1. Let go and let God.

You have to learn how to step out of the way and allow God to be who He is. Learn to depend wholly on Him if you want to see God manifest for you in His fullness.

"We felt we were doomed to die and saw how powerless we were to help ourselves, but that was good, for then we put everything into the hands of God, who alone could save us, for he can even raise the dead." (2 Corinthians 1:8-9 (LB))

2. Start your day with gratitude.

Every day you sleep and wake up, realize that someone else has died. If you are alive, it's all by the mercies of God. That means you need to appreciate God regularly. In fact, the best way to start your day is with a deep sense of gratitude. "My voice shalt thou hear in the morning, O LORD; in the morning will I direct my prayer unto thee, and will look up." (Psalm 5:3 (KJV))

The Psalmist declared, "This is the day which the LORD hath made; we will rejoice and be glad in it." (Psalm 118:24 (KJV)). Never get to the point in your life where you begin to disregard God's mercy upon your life. Life is a very precious gift, and it should never be taken for granted.

3. Believe that something wonderful is going to happen.

If you want to experience something extraordinary, believe in it. Don't be negative, no matter the negativity that surrounds you. Adding negativity to negativity is simply suicide. Instead, focus on the good, expect the good, and you will have it good.

"And we know that all things work together for good to them that love God, to them who are the called according to his purpose." (Romans 8:28 (KJV))

"Being confident of this very thing, that he which hath begun a good work in you will perform it until the day of Jesus Christ:" (Philippians 1:6 (KJV))

Every time things are really tough, and you want to have a beautiful experience, show God that you trust Him regardless of the prevailing circumstances. Don't look unto man, but unto God.

"Blessed is the man that trusteth in the LORD, and whose hope the LORD is. For he shall be as a tree planted by the waters, and that spreadeth out her roots by the river, and shall not see when heat cometh, but her leaf shall be green; and shall not be careful in the year of drought, neither shall cease from yielding fruit." (Jeremiah 17:7-8 (KJV))

4. Focus always on the end rewards.

Never focus on the present alone. Yes, you may be experiencing all kinds of trouble, but focus on the possibilities of the future, not on the limitations of the present. You may not see all your dreams come true now, but you can see them in your mind's eyes.

"That is what is meant by the Scriptures which say that no mere man has ever seen, heard, or even imagined what wonderful things God has ready for those who love the Lord." (1 Corinthians 2:9 (LB))

"Beloved, now are we the sons of God, and it doth not yet appear what we shall be: but we know that, when he shall appear, we shall be like him; for we shall see him as he is." (1 John 3:2 (KJV))

You can have a beautiful life, but not with a negative mindset. If you choose to focus on the positive side of everything by engaging the law of belief, you will live a life beyond the ordinary.

Chapter Three

The Law of Expectation

In life, we attract what we expect. It is your expectation that determines your experience. If you expect things to turn out right, they will; if you expect things to turn south, that is almost exactly what will happen. Whatever you expect with confidence becomes your self-fulfilling prophecy. In other words, they are bound to come to pass. This is technically called the law of expectation. Your expectations greatly influence your life, including your relationship, health, career, and finances. It impacts how you look at your future. It affects how you look at others and how you look at God. Your expectations will affect how you view the world, how you view success or failure, and how you respond to situations, especially adverse circumstances.

The expectation is the mind's drawing power, which acts in the invisible realm and brings the impossible to manifestation. Your expectation is a belief that something will happen or is likely to happen; it is a feeling or thought about how successful someone or something will be. Your expectations refer to your target or your goals. It will go a long way towards determining whether you will be happy.

Thought is the prerequisite to everything. Our lives tend to travel in the direction of our strongest thoughts. In other words, your thoughts have a tremendous impact on your life. Therefore, our ability to originate strong thoughts and mentally move in a thought-filled world is our guarantee of abundant life. The good news is that, as children of God, we have access to everything we need to live victoriously and triumphantly. All we need to do is to let God have his way. Remember, His fountains never run dry.

Re-navigate

As a child of God, you must learn to turn your expectations toward God. I know that God usually uses men and women as our channel of blessing, but He remains our ultimate source. So, rather than looking up to human beings, who are only channels, look unto God, your source, expecting Him to bless you. Thank God for all the beautiful people God has surrounded you with, but if you can look beyond them and put your trust in God, you will find every beautiful thing you may desire—new strength, blessings, favor, love, joy, peace, happiness, victory, and abundance.

God is a spiritual fountain from which all the visible and invisible come. This fountain can never be depleted. Every created order emanated from Him. In the book of Genesis, chapter 1, we understand that God created the heavens and the earth in the beginning. Where was God before He created the heavens, earth, angels, thrones, trees, etc.? Where was He? Of course, he was in eternity.

Then, the next question is, where were heaven, earth, and everything made with them before the beginning? The answer to these questions is found in understanding the very nature of God. God is the creator, the self-existent one, omniscient, omnipotent, and omnipresent. In other words, he can do anything, at any time, with or without anyone involved. So, when He was ready to have heaven and earth and everything He eventually created, He simply spoke them into being. He is the Almighty, the all-sufficient One. He is sufficient in Himself and does not need anybody's input to be who He is or do what He does. That means God plus nothing equals enough. You don't have to add anything to Him to get the right mix you need—because He is more than enough.

Your confidence will be very high when you have such a personality as your source. You won't have to be bothered about anything because He is more than capable of making anything possible for you. That will make your expectations concrete and your desires sure. God's spirit is always omnipresent and stands ready to help you.

Redefining Your Boundary

One of the reasons expectations are powerful is that they define the boundaries of your blessings. If your expectations are small, your results will be small; if your expectations are "big," your results will be big, reflecting the size of your expectations.

There are three fundamental principles we need to understand about our expectations:

1. God will use what we give him.

Our expectations are the starting point of our miracles. For instance, in the story of Elisha and the widow of Zarephath, her husband had died, leaving a huge pile of debts, enough to turn his sons into slaves. But then, she ran to Elisha to seek help. Of course, Elisha asked what she had in her house. It was just a little pot of oil. Then Elisha gave her a prophetic instruction to go and borrow as many vessels as she could and start pouring into them, after which she could sell the oil and get money to pay off the debt:

"Now there cried a certain woman of the wives of the sons of the prophets unto Elisha, saying, thy servant my husband is dead, and thou knowest that thy servant did fear the Lord: and the creditor is come to take unto him my two sons to be bondmen. And Elisha said unto her, what shall I do for thee? Tell me, what hast thou in the house? And she said, thine handmaid hath not anything in the house, save a pot of oil. Then he said, Go, borrow thee vessels abroad of all thy neighbors, even empty vessels; borrow not a few. And when thou art come in, thou shalt shut the door upon thee and upon thy sons, and shalt pour out into all those vessels, and thou shalt set aside that which is full. So, she went from him; and shut the door upon her and upon her sons, who brought the vessels to her, and she poured out. And it came to pass, when the vessels were full, that she said unto her son, Bring me yet a vessel. And he said unto her, There is not a vessel more. And the oil stayed. Then she came and told the man of God. And he said, Go, sell the oil, and pay thy debt, and live thou and thy children of the rest." (2 Kings 4:1-7 (KJV))

After she had obeyed and began to pour the oil, to her amazement, the little oil just kept multiplying until every available vessel was exhausted. Although the power of God moved tremendously through the prophet Elisha, the containers provided by the woman limited the flow of the oil (blessing). As soon as the last vessel he had was filled, the oil flow ceased. What does that tell us? Even though God was limitless in his capacity to keep the oil flowing, the capacity of that woman's vessels was insufficient to contain all the possibilities God had placed on her little cruise of oil.

Of course, she soon found out that the supply was shut off. There was not a drop left. She was only able to receive as much oil as she had expected. This could be likened to the limit of her expectations as measured by the number of vessels she had collected. She got only what she had deeply expected. If she had expected more, she would have had more.

The point is this: God can only do for you what you expect Him to do for you. God is only ready to give what man is ready to receive. If your expectations mark you as unready, you will miss out on what God intends for you. Ultimately, the widow received more from the Lord than she had asked for. She got much more than she had bargained for. Her request was only that her sons be delivered from lives of servitude. But God gave her much more, just like the book of Ephesians promised:

"Now unto Him, that is able to do exceedingly abundantly above all that we ask or think, according to the power that worketh in us." (Ephesians 3:20 (KJV))

We can accomplish the impossible when we see the invisible. It has been said that Moses had his eyes on God ("By faith he forsook Egypt, not fearing the wrath of the king; for he endured, as seeing him who is invisible." Hebrews 11:27. Because he focused on God, Moses could see Him, who is impossible to see. This is the key to a miracle— keeping your eyes on God, not the problem. Expect the best and strive to become your best. If you can trust Him, who is invisible, you will enjoy His blessings endlessly!

2. God can take a little bit and multiply it.

The ability of God is always expressed in a supernatural act. The supernatural is God's "super" on your "natural" efforts, giving you a supernatural advantage. One of the ways you know that God is with you is by what you can accomplish with little. Samson could kill a thousand Philistines with the jawbone of an ass. That was supernatural. David killed Goliath with a slingshot (1 Samuel 17). That was purely supernatural. In the same vein, God can take something insignificant and make something great and beautiful out of it. And one of the ways He does this is by multiplying small amounts into large amounts, as we saw with the widow (2 Kings 4:1-7). All you need to do is to put a seed in His hand. When you put something as little as a seed into the hand of God, He will simply take it and multiply it back to you.

When Jesus was going to feed the multitude, He simply took five loaves of bread and two fish and multiplied them.

"And when he had taken the five loaves and the two fishes, he looked up to heaven, and blessed, and brake the loaves, and gave them to his disciples to set before them; and the two fishes divided He among them all." (Mark 6:41 (KJV))

And the beautiful thing is that after the multitude was full, there was a significant leftover of both bread and fish. God is the God of abundance; He never leaves little as it is; He is a master at turning little into greatness (Ephesians 3:20).

3. Look to God as your infinite supply.

When you realize that God can multiply whatever you place in His hand, you will learn to look to him for your supply. The amazing thing is that He not only multiplies what you give to Him, but He has a grand plan for your destiny. He cares so much about us that He has designed a great life for every one of us, His children. His plan for us is the most beautiful plan you can think of—a plan to give us an expected end:

"For I know the thoughts that I think toward you, saith the LORD, thoughts of peace, and not of evil, to give you an expected end." (Jeremiah 29:11 (KJV))

No wonder the prophet, Jeremiah, boldly declared:

"Blessed is the man that trusteth in the Lord, and whose

hope the Lord is. For he shall be as a tree planted by the waters, and that spreadeth out her roots by the river, and shall not see when heat cometh, but her leaf shall be green; and shall not be careful in the year of drought, neither shall cease from yielding fruit." (Jeremiah 17:7-8 (KJV))

However, until you look to God and completely trust Him as the source of your supply, you will continue to be a victim of the difficulties that others face. Do not put yourself under the same adverse circumstances as those who do not know God.

It Takes a Burning Desire

As a general principle, a burning desire will always translate into outstanding accomplishments. A desire is something you expect to achieve. However, if you choose not to sustain any desires or expectations, you will have no significant accomplishments. Without a burning desire, you cannot remain persistent until you see your desires come through, especially when there are obstacles in your path or when you face life-threatening circumstances or a tragedy. When you have a burning desire, your perspective on adversity changes drastically. In fact, rather than seeing the adversity, you will see the opportunities it could unlock. "Delight thyself also in the Lord, and he shall give thee the desires of thine heart." (Psalm 37:4 (KJV))

Despite temporary setbacks, it took a burning desire to keep Thomas A. Edison working on his incandescent light experiment. It took a burning desire to keep him in business when tragedy struck. When Thomas Edison was sixty-seven years old, a great fire burned down his famous laboratory in New Jersey. And not only did he lose several million dollars in his equipment, but he also lost the records for most of his life's work. However, the following day, he walked out by the charred embers and said, "There is great value in disaster. All our mistakes are burned up. Thank God we can start anew." He turned an apparent stumbling block into a steppingstone.

The lesson from the story is that we should always look for the good in every situation in life. So, rather than focusing on the mountain, we focus on the little mustard seed of faith, which is capable of eliminating any mountain.

Secondly, obstacles viewed from a higher perspective are valuable steppingstones to success. Remember, we were made to conquer, rise above obstacles, and demonstrate God's divine abilities on our side. We should rise with the "I can do it attitude" and win, despite any obstacle we may face on the path of life. Apostle Paul declared, "I can do all things through Christ which strengtheneth me." (Philippians 4:13 (KJV))

And that is only possible when you have a burning desire--a desire strong enough to drown any obstacle you may face in life. If you expect the best, if you demand the best, you will have the best. This is a powerful law of life. Your expectation determines your manifestation. In the words of William Carrie, "expect great things from

God, and attempt great things for God, because that brings honor to Him." It won't be long before you are reckoned among the great if you do.

Chapter Four

Discipline Your Expectations

It is not enough to have expectations; you need to discipline your expectations and get to the point where you bring your expectations under strict rules. That is the only time you gain the power to turn your expectations into a reality. Without discipline, your expectations will die as expectations and never come to pass.

Discipline refers to behavior that shows a willingness to obey rules or orders. The Bible, in showing the importance of discipline, says:

"He that hath no rule over his own spirit is like a city that is broken down, and without walls." (Proverbs 25:28 (KJV))

It is impossible to become great without discipline. Every great success story is usually a product of great discipline. If you want to know what differentiates the successful and great from the unsuccessful people of this world, it is discipline. When you see two individuals with the same level of opportunities, knowledge, and relationships, the difference in their results will be traceable to their level of discipline. It takes great discipline both to acquire relevant knowledge and apply it. If you master discipline, you have mastered yourself and have mastered life.

There are two basic pains in life: the pain of discipline and the pain of regret. The pain of discipline prevents the pain of regret. The pain of discipline is simply the pain you have to go through while paying the price of greatness. Once you decide to follow your destiny of greatness in God, you automatically subscribe to the pain of discipline, the discipline to learn, grow, and develop the character and skills required to fulfill your destiny. And I must say, it takes great pain to be who you need to be, do what you need to do, and then have what you need to have. It takes pain, and until you are ready to shoulder this pain, forget about the greatness you dream of. And the reason is simple: everything you need is on the other side of your growth.

Growth comes with a lot of pains. It takes a lot of pain to wake up early, work all night long, read all the books you need to read and sacrifice your limited resources to acquire the skills required for your next level. It takes a lot of pain to delay gratification and put your very best work into what you do.

On the other hand, regret is the pain and disappointment you feel when you get to the end of your life only to find out that you lived below your potential. When you get to the end of your life only to discover how many things you missed because you were either afraid of taking steps, making sacrifices, taking risks, or waiting for other people's approval before you could act. I mean, that is a great and unbearable pain to go through. And the most unfortunate thing is that it would be too late at that time. You would know exactly what was at stake but would lack the capacity to make amends.

Regret is why many people strongly wish they could turn back the hands of time at the end of their lives. This is a very terrible place to be. And for you to avoid the excruciating pain of regret, you need to make hay while the sun shines; you need to be willing to bear the pain of discipline. It would help if you disciplined yourself to do what it takes to be all you were created to be. Everyone will be judged by what they did in their lifetime and through their generation. It is your turn, just like David, to serve your generation.

"For David, after he had served his own generation by the will of God, fell on sleep, and was laid unto his fathers, and saw corruption." (Acts 13:36 (KJV))

When your time on earth is up, whether you sleep peacefully and joyfully, like David, will be determined by whether or not you accepted Jesus Christ as your Lord and Savior. But right next to that would be what you did with your life. You will experience eternal joy based on whether you were daring enough to do all God assigned you. It will be influenced by whether or not you made a difference in your world. But you know what, that requires great discipline.

It takes discipline to be great. If you want to be the best, if you're going to be victorious, if you're going to be great or win in life, you have to pay the price of discipline. Let discipline and expectation become your shield.

Truly, the proof of your expectations is in the steps you are taking in the direction of that expectation. If you have no discipline, you have no expectations. Remember, where there is no vision, the people perish. One translation says that the people cast off restraint where there is no vision. The word restraint is the same word as a discipline. That means that discipline proves that you have a vision or expectation. In other words, you can't be sleeping, wasting time all day, and expect to achieve your dreams. It's practically impossible!

You become great by committing yourself to something bigger than yourself and exercising discipline to accomplish that end. When you commit to something (a vision) bigger than yourself, that vision will impose discipline on you, positioning you to achieve your objectives. Remember, the more disciplined you are, the stronger your character and rewards will be.

Four Attributes to Adopt to Discipline Your Expectations

Now here are the four attributes to adapt to discipline your expectations:

1. Have a disciplined mentality.

If you truly want to discipline your expectations, you

need to have a disciplined mentality. You need to have a mindset that supports and promotes discipline as a prerequisite for results. This was what enabled Paul to stand out from the crowd. Even though he was not one of the disciples who walked the streets of Israel with Jesus, he earned a unique and exceptional place in the kingdom of God.

Today we all talk about the fact that he wrote two-thirds of the entire New Testament, a feat that he gave glory to God for, yet we cannot fail to realize how much effort he put into its realization. Paul gave us one of the secrets by which he could accomplish all that. He said it took severe discipline. He referred to a level of discipline that he compared to an athlete running for a medal.

You know, it's one thing to practice for fun and another to practice for a medal. If you are truly running for a gold medal, you had better be serious. You have to have a level of discipline that prepares, propels, and positions you to win such a medal. Here is how he puts it:

"Know ye not that they which run in a race run all, but one receiveth the prize? So run, that ye may obtain. And every man that striveth for the mastery is temperate in all things. Now they do it to obtain a corruptible crown, but we an incorruptible. I therefore so run, not as uncertainly; so fight I, not as one that beateth the air: But I keep under my body, and bring it into subjection: lest that by any means, when I have preached to others, I myself should be a castaway." (1 Corinthians 9:24-27 (KJV)). I like the way it is rendered in the New Living Translation (NLT):

"Don't you realize that in a race, everyone runs, but only one person gets the prize? So run to win! All athletes are disciplined in their training. They do it to win a prize that will fade away, but we do it for an eternal prize." (1 Corinthians 9:24-27 (NLT))

What Paul was doing was comparing the Christian life to sports. First, he talked about running. He said that winning in your Christian life, just as in the field of sports, depends on discipline. Sports stars win primarily because of their ability to persevere in the face of adversity, and, of course, they are motivated by the gold medal in front of them. And for such a physical victory, they are willing to go through whatever it takes to achieve their goal or expectation.

It's a Fight!

On the other hand, he describes the Christian life as a fight—which requires discipline. "I therefore so run, not as uncertainly; so, fight I, not as one that beateth the air."

When you go to the book of Timothy, he describes our Christian life as a fight of faith.

"Fight the good fight of faith, lay hold on eternal life, whereunto thou art also called, and hast professed a good profession before many witnesses." (1 Timothy 6:12 (KJV))

Now, whether it's a run or a fight, discipline is what is required. This way, the Bible talks about the narrow way leading to life.

"Because strait is the gate, and narrow is the way, which

leadeth unto life, and few there be that find it." (Matthew 7:14 (KJV))

2. You must practice disciplined behaviors.

It will not be as effective as having a disciplined mentality. Having a disciplined mindset is only the starting point. You need to put it to work by practicing disciplined behavior. The Bible reveals the difference between being willing and being obedient.

"If ye be willing and obedient, ye shall eat the good of the land:" (Isaiah 1:19 (KJV))

It is one thing to have the willingness or the mindset to do something and another thing to do it. Haven't you seen people who make fantastic promises but never lift a finger to fulfill them? If you have the mindset, it's only natural that you should back it up with corresponding behavior.

3. Keep your eyes on the result.

To remain disciplined, you need your eyes to focus on your result. You cannot take your eyes off your expected outcomes. If you do, not only will you be distracted, your discipline and your drive will wane, thereby compromising your vision or expectations. Paul's behavior was motivated by his expectation of a future reward from God.

"I have fought a good fight, I have finished my course, I have kept the faith: Henceforth there is laid up for me a crown of righteousness, which the Lord, the righteous judge, shall give me at that day: and not to me only, but unto all them also that love his appearing." (2 Timothy 4:7-8 (KJV))

"Therefore, since we are surrounded by such a great cloud of witnesses, let us throw off everything that hinders and the sin that so easily entangles. And let us run with perseverance the race marked out for us." (Hebrews 12:1-3 (NLT))

Even Jesus operated by this rule. He did not proceed to the cross just because he had to; he joyously went because of the joy (expectation) before him. Part of that joy came from seeing you and me, not just saved, sanctified, and filled with the Holy Spirit but fully representing Him in all aspects of life.

"Fixing our eyes on Jesus, the pioneer and perfecter of faith. For the joy set before Him, he endured the cross, scorning its shame, and sat down at the right hand of the throne of God. Consider him who endured such opposition from sinners so that you will not grow weary and lose heart." (Hebrews 12:1-3 (NLT))

4. Your spiritual supply will never be depleted.

In the previous chapter, we emphasized that God is our source. Your supply will never run dry if the almighty God is your source. Remember, God is always more than enough to exceed all your expectations, regardless of what they are.

"Now unto him, that is able to do exceeding abundantly above all that we ask or think, according to the power that worketh in us." (Ephesians 3:20 (KJV))

Here are a few more scriptural proofs of the abundant, nature, and capacity of God:

"But my God shall supply all your need according to his

riches in glory by Christ Jesus." (Philippians 4:19 KJV))

"The LORD is my shepherd; I shall not want." (Psalm 23:1 (KJV))

"The earth is the LORD's, and the fullness thereof; the world, and they that dwell therein. For he hath founded it upon the seas, and established it upon the floods." (Psalm 24:1-2 (KJV))

"The LORD shall command the blessing upon thee in thy storehouses, and in all that thou settest thine hand unto, and he shall bless thee in the land which the LORD thy God giveth thee." (Deuteronomy 28:8 (KJV))

The amazing thing is that God does not only have more than enough resources that we need, but He is also willing to give them to his children. It says, if you are willing and obedient, you shall eat the good of the land (Isaiah 1:19).

Expect the Move of God

A new era is here! The season of new wine is here. Rise to the belief, the faith, and the expectation that you want to experience God's power and blessings in your life like never before. His hands are wide open! Jesus said in Matthew 9:17, "neither do men put new wine into old bottles: else the bottles break, and the wine runneth out, and the bottles perish: but they put new wine into new bottles, and both are preserved."

Wine is symbolic of the Holy Spirit.

Ephesians 5:18 "and be not drunk with wine, wherein is excess; but be filled with the holy spirit."

If you really expect God to move on your behalf, you will get a new wineskin as evidence of your expectation. While expectations are important, they should be supported by a life of discipline. Otherwise, you will be disappointed. In other words, it will not come to pass. But I pray for you, your expectations shall not be cut short!

Chapter Five

Dare To Dream

A dream is the starting point of every significant achievement in life. All known inventions, creativity, and products began as an idea or a dream in someone's heart. Without a dream, faith will remain dormant. But with an extraordinary dream comes the inspiration to believe in God and seek the dream's realization.

According to the Merriam-Webster dictionary, a dream is an idea or vision created in your imagination and is not real. It also refers to something you have wanted to do, be, or have for a long time. It is the picture of a preferable future for life, an organization, or a nation.

Therefore, a dream is a beacon of hope amid hopelessness. One of the powers of a dream is its ability to unlock your faith. A dream on the inside of you will not only quicken your faith but also position you to see its manifestation.

"Therefore, I say unto you, What things soever ye desire when ye pray, believe that ye receive them, and ye shall have them." (Mark 11:24 (KJV))

"Now faith is the substance of things hoped for, the evidence of things not seen." (Hebrew 11:1 (KJV))

Faith is what substantiates our hope. Hope here represents a dream, desire, vision, expectation, or aspiration in someone's heart, which will realize its objectives when pursued.

Not Without a Dream

You cannot make headway in life by being complacent. One of the keys to progress is dissatisfaction with your present level. It's excellent and scriptural to be content with what you have, but it is also scriptural to desire something better than where you presently are. Being content does not mean you should be complacent. You have to have a dream for your next level. You will not experience a significant change in your life without a dream and aspirations.

You cannot afford to live a life without a dream. Real poverty is not a lack of money; real poverty is a lack of dreams. When a person lacks a dream, their life will lack meaning and significance. In Proverbs 29, the Bible says, "Where there is no vision, the people perish: but he that keepeth the law, happy is he." In other words, where there is no dream, life goal, objective, purpose, or strong aim, people perish.

Dream and Hunger

Without a dream, you will not be hungry enough for a higher level of your life; you will not go after your next level of growth in your business. Only those who are hungry are entitled to be filled.

Matthew 5:6 says, "Blessed are they which do hunger and thirst after righteousness: for they shall be filled."

Without a deep-seated hunger and craving, you will not realize your dreams. Everywhere dreams come true, whether in the Bible or in our world today, it is essential because someone was hungry enough to go after their dreams.

Blind but Hungry

A particular incident happened in the scriptures, which is a testament to the power of hunger in fulfilling a dream. It was about the man most people refer to as "blind Bartimaeus." He had been blind for a long time. But when he heard that Jesus was passing by, he started crying desperately for help.

"And they came to Jericho: and as he went out of Jericho with his disciples and a great number of people, blind Bartimaeus, the son of Timaeus, sat by the highway side begging. And when he heard that it was Jesus of Nazareth, he began to cry out and say, Jesus, thou Son of David, have mercy on me. And many charged him that he should hold his peace: but he cried the more a great deal, Thou Son of David, have mercy on me." (Mark 10:46-48 (KJV))

Although people tried to stop him, some people told him to shut up; he persisted. The more they tried to stop him, the louder he cried until he got the attention of the master.

"And Jesus stood still and commanded him to be called. And they call the blind man, saying unto him, Be of good comfort, rise; he calleth thee. And he, casting away his garment, rose and came to Jesus. And Jesus answered and said unto him, What wilt thou that I should do unto thee? The blind man said unto him, Lord, that I might receive my sight. And Jesus said unto him, Go thy way; thy faith hath made thee whole. And immediately he received his sight, and followed Jesus in the way." (Mark 10: 49-52 (KJV))

He didn't care what the crowd thought or felt. He would not compromise his dream of receiving his sight because someone along the road tried to discourage him. His hunger eventually paid off.

If you want to see your dream; come true, you better be ready to do what the blind Bartimaeus did. He cried desperately for help. And I can tell you, we all need to get that kind of attitude—a desperate hunger to pursue our dreams. He wanted to receive his sight at all costs, and receive it, he did!

The Portrait of a Dreamer

An excellent example of a dreamer in the scriptures is Joseph. Joseph began to dream about being highly influential in society right from his youth. He saw his future way ahead of time.

"And Joseph dreamed a dream, and he told it his brethren: and they hated him yet the more. And he said unto them, Hear, I pray you, this dream which I have dreamed: For, behold, we were binding sheaves in the field, and, lo, my sheaf arose, and also stood upright; and, behold, your sheaves stood round about, and made obeisance to my sheaf." (Genesis 37:5-7 (KJV))

Although he went through a lot of challenging times, it was his dream that eventually brought him to prominence. Dreamers rule the world. Don't live without a dream. And like Joseph, your dream will make way for you.

As Far as You Can See

Your dream is what determines the size of your destiny. What God will do in your life is as far as you can see. The promise of God to you has no future without a dream. God had promised to make Abraham the father of many nations (Genesis 12:2). But Abraham could not see the fulfillment of that promise without a dream. He did not have a child. God looked at him and saw his frustration; He knew that nothing would change unless Abraham could conceive the dream of fathering many nations. So, He had to intervene by revealing this principle of a dream to him.

"And the Lord said unto Abram, after that Lot was separated from him, Lift up now thine eyes, and look from the place where thou art northward, and southward, and eastward, and westward: For all the land which thou seest, to thee will I give it, and to thy seed forever. And I will make thy seed as the dust of the earth: so that if a man can number the dust of the earth, then shall thy seed also be numbered." (Genesis 13:14-17 (KJV))

That was when Abraham finally conceived the dream of fathering many nations. Amazingly, it's never too late to dream. It was at age seventy-five that God gave Abraham a dream. Nothing will change without a dream. It didn't change anything for Abraham until he saw it. It was his dream that made the difference.

If you can conceive a dream and believe it, you can achieve it. Those who believe this focus on possibilities, not on limitations. Regardless of what is against you, you can when you believe you can. But to dream effectively and believe in seeing them actualized, here are a few things you need to do:

1. Remember what God can do.

If you can remember what God can do, your faith will be alive. And one of the ways to remember what God can do is to meditate on His word. His word is what reveals to us what He can do. His word tells us that all things are possible with Him. And if we believe Him, all things become possible for us.

"But Jesus beheld them, and said unto them, With men this is impossible, but with God all things are possible." (Matthew 19:26 (KJV))

2. Rely on God's promises.

God's words remain the boundary of his commitment to man, so relying on His promises is the most authentic way to secure his interventions in the issues of our lives and realize our dreams.

"Who against hope believed in hope, that he might become the father of many nations, according to that which was spoken, So shall thy seed be." (Romans 4:18 (KJV))

3. Identify the truth and believe it.

It is your responsibility to go through the Scripture and locate the truths that align with the areas of your need. And as you meditate on them, faith will erupt from your heart. That is the starting point of all miracles.

"And the Word was made flesh, and dwelt among us, (and we beheld his glory, the glory as of the only begotten of the Father, full of grace and truth." (John 1:14 (KJV))

4. Rejoice.

A person of faith always rejoices in the promises of God. Joy is not just a way to demonstrate faith; it is also the key to drawing from the wells of God's blessings as made available through Christ's death. Joy and praise are what you do when you are truly persuaded.

"And being fully persuaded that, what he had promised, he was able also to perform." (Romans 4:21 (KJV))

Dreams help you break all the barriers to your faith and progress. You can be anything, do anything, and have anything you see in your imagination. And the beautiful thing about it is that if you hold those pictures long enough in your mind and begin to pursue them one by one, they will begin to come to pass. It's all a matter of time. Learn to dream, expect the best, have a life goal, have a vision, and you will see your faith erupt into a new dimension!

Chapter Six

Speaking Words of Power

Your capacity to believe determines everything else in your life. Anything God can do, your faith in God can do. If you have real unwavering faith, you can move any mountain. In other words, you can have victory in the circumstances of life. This kind of faith can be seen through your words or your actions. Many people know about the action part, but very few realize the part words play in the operation of their faith.

One primary indication that you believe is through what you are saying. There is no genuine faith without the words of faith. The speaking side of faith comes even before the action side of faith. However, both of them are equally important. You have to believe it and say it, and then you proceed to take actions to bring into manifestation what you have been saying.

"Have faith in God. For verily I say unto you, that whosoever shall say unto this mountain, be thou removed, and be thou cast into the sea; and shall not doubt in his heart, but shall believe that those things which he saith shall come to pass; he shall have whatsoever he saith." (Mark 11:23-24 (KJV))

You Have What You Say

Whatever you believe and declare with your mouth will become your reality. If you can say it, you can have it; otherwise, you won't. Anything too big for your mouth will be too big for your life. You need the audacity of faith to say what God has spoken to become all you were created to be. Your greatest undoing is your failure to believe and your lack of boldness to declare what you believe. You have to be audacious enough to say everything God says about you; it is only in so doing will you realize your dreams. Your life will expand to the size of your faith confession and shrink to the level of your doubt, unbelief, and confession. If you want a great life and commands vast results, it begins with your mouth.

If you want to be a person of unwavering faith, your words must reflect that. You can't have one thing in your heart and another in your mouth.

Here is something you must understand: Faith is not just a belief system; faith is a spirit, and the spirit of faith is a talking spirit. You don't just believe and keep mute.

"We having the same spirit of faith, according as it is written, I believed, and therefore have I spoken; we also believe, and therefore speak." (2 Corinthians 4:13 (KJV))

Even with salvation, your mouth is required; when you believe in your heart and confess with your mouth, then you are saved.

"That if thou shalt confess with thy mouth the Lord Jesus, and shalt believe in thine heart that God hath raised him from the dead, thou shalt be saved. For with the heart, man believeth unto righteousness, and with the mouth, confession is made unto salvation." (Romans 10:9,10 (KJV))

Your confession will bring you into the reality of your desires; your confession will bring you possession. It is, therefore, not enough to believe the word of God in your heart alone; you have to confess it with your mouth to have it. The same way you receive salvation is how you receive everything else from God. Yes, the provision has been made, but you have to accept the responsibility to unleash your faith via the words of your mouth.

There is Power

And believe me, there is power in the words of your mouth. There is creative power in the words of your mouth to turn all your possibilities into reality. Everything God ever created, he created with words. The first chapter of Genesis is a testament to the creative power of words.

"In the beginning, God created the heaven and the earth. And the earth was without form and void, and darkness was upon the face of the deep. And the Spirit of God moved upon the face of the waters. And God said, "Let there be light: and there was light. And God saw the light, that it was good: and God divided the light from the darkness. And God called the light Day, and the darkness he called Night. And the evening and the morning were the first day." (Genesis 1:1-5 (KJV))

Every time God spoke, it was followed by the emergence of physical reality. That was how He created the trees, the sun, the moon, stars, fishes, and the list goes on and on and on. In other words, the creative energy is communicated through words. Words are powerful!

Words are power containers; they convey and transport, like a vehicle, whatever you put into them. So, my friend, put life, prosperity, and health into words. Let your words be your errand boy and your forerunner by which you preempt the future and create the reality you desire. You are a tree of righteousness, and your words are your fruit. Even your very satisfaction comes from the very words of your mouth.

"A man's belly shall be satisfied with the fruit of his mouth, and with the increase of his lips shall he be filled. Death and life are in the power of the tongue: and they that love it shall eat the fruit thereof." (Proverbs 18:20-21 (KJV))

Your experiences are scheduled by the words that come out of your mouth. Beware of what you say because it decides the direction and quality of your life. If your experiences are bad, check your words. If everything around you is dying, it may be because you're speaking of death.

Your words are the raw material from which you are building your life. Words are seeds you sow into your career, health, relationship, business, future, and destiny. If you don't like the harvest, change the seed you are sowing. You cannot be speaking trash and expect your life to produce treasure; no, you get what you say. You cannot be talking about sickness, poverty, and death and expect to experience the abundant life that the Scriptures promise. Therefore, stop speaking negative and doubtful words and start speaking positive, faith-filled words.

Your Confession is Your Judgment

Your life is never dependent on what someone else says about you but on what you say about yourself. You should never let someone else's opinion become your reality. But with your mouth, you can chart your life course. It is your words that decide your judgment. The children of Israel, who were privileged to experience the power of God demonstrated to deliver them from Egypt, eventually perished in the desert, all because they spoke the wrong words. They used their tongues to seal their fate—in the negative direction. God's response to their spoken words was this:

"...As truly as I live, saith the Lord, as ye have spoken in mine ears, so will I do to you." (Numbers 14:28 (KJV))

In Matthew's gospel, the Bible puts it this way:

"For by thy words thou shalt be justified, and by thy words, thou shalt be condemned." (Mathew 12:37 (KJV))

Your Acknowledgment

Your confession acknowledges who you are, what you have, and what you can do in Christ. I love the way the apostle Paul puts it in the book of Philemon.

"That the communication of thy faith may become effectual by the acknowledging of every good thing which is in you in Christ Jesus." (Philemon 1:6 (KJV))

When you say, "By His stripes, I am healed. I am strong. I refuse to be sick, or greater is he that is me than he that is in the world..." what you are doing is that you are both acknowledging, as well as appropriating, what belongs to you. Healing belongs to you; prosperity, health, protection, and all the beautiful fruits of redemption are yours. And it all starts with you; they are yours, and they are appropriated by the words you speak.

On the other hand, your confession is your agreement with God. When you boldly confess or declare your possibilities in Christ, you agree with God. Confession is the Greek word "homology," which means speaking the same thing with consent. And when you speak the same thing in agreement with God's word, you will begin to get results like God.

Are You Afloat or Drowning?

You either drown or stay afloat with the words of your mouth. Your words reveal whether you are gravitating north or south. To the north, you are bouncing back, and to the south, it means you are sinking deeper and deeper. Unfortunately, many people are caught up in negativity through their words. I sincerely acknowledge that sometimes it's easier to say negative things than positive ones because that makes sense.

It doesn't make sense to disregard your physical condition and speak of your spiritual possibilities most of the time. It seems more natural to declare your feelings or experiences instead of God's word. With the current pandemic and its indirect impact on people's economies, many would rather be politically correct than biblically correct. They would instead declare their facts than proclaim their faith in God. This is a huge concern, but it's true. But may I remind you that your faith in God is not a disadvantage or a liability? Your faith in God is a priceless treasure for your benefit. Publicly and privately confessing your faith is one of the most important contributions you can make in these challenging times.

It Will Be Worth it

In the wake of the current global events occasioned by the pandemic, with men's hearts failing them, there is no better time to invest in your faith than now. There is a lot of hopelessness, despair, fear, and depression, and many people are already on the verge of a nervous breakdown. Mental health concerns have suddenly hit an all-time high. And so, there has never been a better time to give attention to your faith than now. And I dare say, you cannot survive the flood of challenges that are likely to occur soon without the life jacket of your faith—and I mean, faith in God, faith in his word, and faith in your faith. You cannot afford to live in doubt now. It is not only a terrible choice but a dangerous one.

We all need faith to thrive and much more, survive, and remain afloat despite adverse situations. And this we will do as we begin to believe and boldly confess God's eternal word.

I tell you what, don't just believe God in your heart, believe Him with your mouth also, by declaring your possibilities with your mouth. If you do that, you will keep yourself and your entire household afloat, but you will also become a beacon of hope to all those around you. Do not join unbelievers or weak believers to speak fear, doubt, and unbelief; instead, choose to be an example of unwavering faith in Jesus Christ. And regardless of how bad things get, hold fast to your confession!

CHAPTER SEVEN

The Place of Prayer

In the arena of faith, prayer is an invaluable asset, and the reason is simply that prayer powers divine revelation, and revelation powers faith. Faith will be alive and strong when prayer is in place, but faith will be weak and ineffective when prayer is lacking. With prayer, you can release your faith and receive your desires. In Mark's gospel, where Jesus himself gave an exposé of the dynamics of faith, He revealed that you could receive what you desire as you believe in it and express it through the medium of prayer.

"Therefore, I say unto you, what things soever ye desire when ye pray, believe that ye receive them, and ye shall have them." (Mark 11:24 (KJV))

However, prayer is not just a medium for releasing your faith. Prayer is also a system for keeping faith active. And the reason is that faith is a spiritual force powered by the power of the Holy Spirit. In other words, as we pray, not only is power activated, but supernatural illumination is also activated, thereby unlocking faith for all possibilities. When faith is alive through prayer, then dreams become a reality.

A Vibrant Prayer Life

Unwavering faith requires a strategic prayer life to keep it working—a prayer life that is vibrant and empowering. An effective prayer life is consistent. Almost everyone known for their faith in the scriptures was also a person of prayer—they were men and women of deep devotion to God. Think about Daniel, who was thrown into the lion's den; how did he overcome such a trial in life? It was simply because he had a vibrant prayer life.

"And I set my face unto the Lord God, to seek by prayer and supplications, with fasting, and sackcloth, and ashes: And I prayed unto the Lord my God..." (Daniel 9:3-4 (KJV))

The Bible encourages a vibrant prayer life for every believer. Regular prayer is supposed to be a part of a believer's lifestyle. If you study the Scriptures, especially where Jesus taught about the subject of prayer, He used the word "when," never "if."

"And when thou prayest, thou shalt not be as the hypocrites are: for they love to pray standing in the synagogues and in the corners of the streets, that they may be seen of men. Verily I say unto you; they have their reward. But thou, when thou prayest, enter into thy closet, and when thou hast shut thy door, pray to thy Father which is in secret; and thy Father which seeth in secret shall reward thee openly." (Matthew 6:5-6 (KJV))

Notice the word "when" clearly stands out in the above passage of Scripture. In other words, vibrant prayer is not optional; you don't choose between praying and not doing it, but you choose "when" to do it. It is, therefore, not enough to pray occasionally; you must develop the habit of prayer. You have to be consistent. There is something about being consistent that keeps your faith on fire.

Jesus, Himself, was a man of prayer. He did not pray occasionally; He maintained a lifestyle of prayer. The Scripture says that He would wake up long before it was day to go and pray.

"And in the morning, rising up a great while before day, he went out, and departed into a solitary place, and there prayed." (Mark 1:35 (KJV))

Jesus was a man of prayer, and because of that, he had so many results. And for that, the multitude thronged around Him every single time He showed up in public. Therefore, his private prayer was the secret of his successful public ministry.

"And Simon and they that were with him followed after him. And when they had found him, they said unto him, all men seek for thee." (Mark 1:36 (KJV))

And because of His level of effectiveness, His disciples asked Him to teach them how to pray.

"And it came to pass, that, as he was praying in a certain place, when he ceased, one of his disciples said unto him, Lord, teach us to pray, as John also taught his disciples." (Luke 11:1 (KJV))

They were amazed at how Jesus healed the sick and performed miraculous signs. But they never asked him to show them how to heal the sick, preach, teach, or even raise the dead; instead, they desperately asked to be taught how to pray. I am sure they finally figured it out. They discovered that his vibrant prayer life was the secret of his faith and power. Prayer is such a powerful spiritual exercise.

The Power to Hear

There is power in prayer to receive guidance from God. Usually, when you start to pray, you immediately open your spiritual receptacles to hear, see, and receive clear direction from God. As a result, Jesus knew what to do each time. Jesus did not just walk out there and begin to heal the sick and raise the dead; He went only where His father directed Him to go, said what God was saying, and healed who God was healing.

"Then answered Jesus and said unto them, Verily, verily, I say unto you, The Son can do nothing of himself, but what he seeth the Father do: for what things soever he doeth, these also doeth the Son likewise. For the Father loveth the Son, and sheweth him all things that himself doeth: and he will shew him greater works than these, that ye may marvel." (John 5:19, 30 (KJV))

Jesus used prayer to activate His discernment into the thoughts, intents, purposes, strategies, and timings of God. His faith was also always alive. Nothing provokes faith in real-time like a "Rhema" word from God. The word "Rhema" is the Greek word for the spoken word.

A Rhema word is also a specific word spoken to a particular person in a particular situation. In other words, if you truly receive a Rhema word from God about what to do about a specific situation, faith will be automatically born in your heart. And I dare say that you don't only receive a Rhema word when you are studying and meditating on the Scriptures; you also receive a Rhema word from God when you are praying. A real-time prayer will cause you to hear God's voice. One of the ways you know whether you are touching the substance at the place of prayer is that your ears and eyes will be open. Prayer is not a monologue, as in speaking to God alone, but a dialogue, as in speaking with God. They are not the same. When you speak with God, you open up a channel for Him to start speaking with you. Effective prayer, therefore, is hearing from God.

"Call unto me, and I will answer thee, and shew thee great and mighty things, which thou knowest not." (Jeremiah 33:3 (KJV))

When you call on God, you have to listen for His response. Many people are not acquainted with this kind of prayer, which explains why they lack significant results in their lives. They are only used to petition and tell God what to do. That kind of prayer is mostly for spiritual babes. But when you begin to mature in the things of God, you will learn how to partner with God. For the most part, your prayers are answered while you are still praying. The Bible says that while you pray, God will answer.

"And it shall come to pass, that before they call, I will answer; and while they are yet speaking, I will hear." (Isaiah 65:24 (KJV))

Whenever we pray, there is a guarantee for answers. God delights in our prayers (Proverbs 15:8 (KJV)).

"If ye shall ask any thing in my name, I will do it." (John 14:14 (KJV))

The amazing thing is that God does not just hear prayers; He hears hearts; He sees and responds to your needs even while you are still thinking about them.

"Now unto him, that is able to do exceeding abundantly above all that we ask or think, according to the power that worketh in us." (Ephesians 3:20 (KJV))

And one of the ways He usually answers is by telling you what to do. He advances you with instruction that will produce whatever you are asking for, and as you execute it, you see the tangible results of your prayers.

God's Ultimate Answer

Any time you are praying and the Spirit of God descends, it is a sign that your prayer has been answered. Remember, God's Spirit is the God of answers. When Elijah finished putting the latter together and praying to God, fire fell from heaven at the mount of Camel. And that is usually how God responds when He has answered.

"And it came to pass at the time of the offering of the evening sacrifice, that Elijah the prophet came near, and said, Lord God of Abraham, Isaac, and of Israel, let it be known this day that thou art God in Israel, and that I am thy servant, and that I have done all these things at thy word. Hear me, O Lord, hear me, that these people may know that thou art the Lord God and that thou hast turned their heart back again. Then the fire of the Lord fell and consumed the burnt sacrifice, and the wood, and the stones, and the dust, and licked up the water that was in the trench." (1 kings 18:36-38 (KJV))

In the book of Revelation, when prayer was offered, God responded by releasing fire, earthquake, and lightning; that was His answer:

"And I saw the seven angels which stood before God, and to them were given seven trumpets. And another angel came and stood at the altar, having a golden censer; and there was given unto him much incense, that he should offer it with the prayers of all saints upon the golden altar which was before the throne. And the smoke of the incense, which came with the prayers of the saints, ascended up before God out of the angel's hand. And the angel took the censer, and filled it with the fire of the altar, and cast it into the earth: and there were voices, and thunderings, and lightning, and an earthquake." (Revelation 8:2-5 (KJV))

When God answers, one of the ways you will know is that there will be the release of His Spirit or anointing in the place of prayer. That supernatural release propels you to take the actions required to convert your desires into their physical manifestation. It is also that supernatural release that eliminates every potential obstacle along your destiny's path.

The Power to Decree

In prayer, you breathe in omnipotence, and you are empowered to make decrees just like God. As powerful as it is, Confession is not as powerful as a faith-filled decree powered from the place of prayer. The difference between confession and Spirit-powered decrees is between hand-throwing a bullet and propelling it from a gun. A hand-thrown bullet could hurt a little bit, depending on the momentum, but a gun-powered bullet is ready to kill. The difference is in the momentum. When words are spoken in the place of prayer, they have creative ability and prophetic ability to cause what is said to happen immediately. This is why God had to allow His Spirit to brood over the surface of the deep before He began to speak words.

"And the earth was without form and void, and darkness was upon the face of the deep. And the Spirit of God moved upon the face of the waters. And God said, let there be light: and there was light. And God saw the light, that it was good." (Genesis 1:2-4 (KJV))

As He spoke into that charged Holy-ghost atmosphere, creation leaped into being. Glory to God! Never underestimate the power of a vibrant prayer to unlock your faith, positioning you for all possibilities. I pray to

God to give you a deeper understanding in this regard.

Chapter Eight

Step Out and Win

Faith is the supernatural power that makes all things possible. Everything you will ever need in your life; healing, protection, deliverance, blessings, peace, breakthrough, prosperity (you name it), is all available to you based on the grace of God (Ephesian 2:8). However, accessing these resources is only possible with absolute faith in God. If you can believe it, you can have whatever you desire.

"Jesus said unto him If thou canst believe, all things are possible to him that believeth." (Mark 9:23 (KJV))

Unfortunately, faith holds no value unless it is accompanied by action. Faith is not faith until it is acted upon. Faith is, therefore, the name of the action you take based on your belief and confidence in the word of God. In other words, faith is action-defined. The primary reason many people do not get the results they desire in life is simply because they don't make moves. Yes, they say they believe, but belief alone is not enough; it must be translated into the corresponding action. Until you move, nothing will move. If you don't begin to take the necessary steps in the direction and dimension of your desires, even your most significant desires will remain an illusion. Remember, faith without works is dead.

"Yea, a man may say, Thou hast faith, and I have works: shew me thy faith without thy works, and I will shew thee my faith by my works. Thou believest that there is one God; thou doest well: the devils also believe and tremble. But wilt thou know, O vain man, that faith without works is dead?" (James 2:18-20,26 (KJV))

Your faith must reflect directly in your actions, and I mean, take actions at the level of the results you desire. You cannot act as an employee and expect to be a great employer of labor. Neither can you be sleeping away your life and claim to be preparing for success in life; success requires diligence. Simply put, your actions must match your desires.

Violent Faith in Action

Jesus was preaching and teaching in a particular place, and we are told that the multitude was so great that there was no space for more people to come in. The entire space inside and outside was filled with people. Today, we would say, there was an overflow crowd outside. There was no way of getting to Jesus. But a particular group of men saw things a little differently. Their friend was very sick and desperately needed urgent supernatural intervention from Jesus. Their actions were how they demonstrated their desperation.

"And it came to pass on a certain day, as he was teaching, that there were Pharisees and doctors of the law sitting by, which were come out of every town of Galilee, and Judaea, and Jerusalem: and the power of the Lord was present to heal them. "And, behold, men brought in a bed a man which was taken with a palsy: and they sought means to bring him in and to lay him before him. And when they could not find by what way they might bring him in because of the multitude, they went upon the housetop and let him down through the tiling with his couch into the midst before Jesus." (Luke 5:17-19 (KJV))

These guys were so desperate to get their friend healed that they were willing to break every protocol and risk their lives to get what they wanted. They ripped the roof off, not minding what anybody would think or say. I am sure they would have encountered resistance from many nay-sayers but deliberately refused to be stopped by them. When they finally got through to Jesus, Jesus stopped and acknowledged their faith publicly: The Bible says Jesus saw their faith:

"And when he saw their faith, he said unto him, Man, thy sins are forgiven thee... (he said unto the sick of the palsy,) I say unto thee, Arise, and take up thy couch, and go into thine house." (Luke 5:20,24 (KJV))

This is one of the most striking images of faith found in the Scripture. To produce the object of faith, faith must be applied to action. Why do you think a farmer goes to his field and works relentlessly and tediously to weed his garden? He knows that weeds will become more assertive and demanding and choke his crops if he doesn't remove them. His faith is evident in his effort.

When Joshua was leading the people of Israel to cross the River Jordan, he was instructed to let the priests carrying the ark of the covenant step into the river first. As the priests stepped into the river and stepped out, it parted in two (Joshua 4:18, (KJV)). If you go through the entire Bible, you will see that nothing changed until people took definite actions.

The faith that says, "upward bound!" is the faith that produces results. That faith is active. You will increase your faith when you accept that your desires are tangible, even though they are in an invisible form.

Faith Opens the Door to the Miraculous

The amazing thing is that once you begin to take the right steps of faith, you will open the door for miracles. Every time faith is truly exercised, a miracle is a natural result. A miracle is a supernatural occurrence that takes place in the natural world. A supernatural occurrence is an occurrence that cannot be explained by science or the laws of nature. In other words, a miracle is beyond the natural, science, and imagination. And faith is the vital connection between the natural and the supernatural.

Whether you study the Bible or history, you will find that every time God moved on earth and did a miracle, it was because somebody dared to believe Him. God has set up the universe governed by laws, some spiritual, others natural. These laws are designed to operate in a hierarchy, meaning that some laws are higher than others. And when a higher law is in effect or puts to work, the lower law will be suspended.

For instance, when you activate the law of lift or floatation, the law of gravity is suspended. That is how it is with spiritual and natural laws. When a spiritual law like faith is activated, natural laws are suspended because spiritual laws are higher than natural laws. Faith is a higher law than the laws of nature; it can do more than the law of physics or any other law. This is how faith creates a miracle: by suspending natural laws. Every time we stretch our faith, a miracle erupts—I mean, every single time.

"Ask, and it shall be given you; seek, and ye shall find; knock, and it shall be opened unto you. For everyone that asketh receiveth; and he that seeketh findeth; and to him that knocketh it shall be opened." (Matthew 7:7-8 (KJV))

Whenever you pray in faith, a miracle is guaranteed. However, where there is no faith, there is no miracle. Unbelief is what short-circuits the power of God in your life. Because of unbelief, Jesus was unable to perform many miracles in His hometown.

"And he did not many mighty works there because of their unbelief." (Matthew 13:58 (KJV))

And the reason is that they knew Him in the flesh; they knew his parents, brothers and sisters, and background, and the result was familiarity and unbelief.

The Bethesda Incidence

Sometimes, to experience a supernatural miracle, you need to step away from the region of familiarity and unbelief. There was a particular incident where Jesus met a blind man who needed a miracle in the city of Bethesda:

"And he cometh to Bethsaida, and they bring a blind man unto him and besought him to touch him. And he took the blind man by the hand and led him out of the town; and when he had spit on his eyes and put his hands upon him, he asked him if he saw ought. And he looked up and said, I see men as trees, walking. After that, he put his hands again upon his eyes and made him look up: and he was restored and saw every man clearly. And he sent him away to his house, saying, neither go into the town nor tell it to any in the town." (Mark 8:22-26 (KJV))

Notice that before Jesus ministered to him, He had to take him by the hand and lead him out of the city. Even after his eyes were miraculously opened, Jesus instructed him not to return to the town, not tell anyone from that city about his miracle. The question is, why did Jesus take him out of the town before he could minister to him? What was it about that city that made miracles almost impossible?

There could be other reasons, but the most likely one is unbelief. Where there is unbelief, the supernatural work of God is often hampered. For us to experience miracles and breakthroughs, God has to remove us from our familiar settings and out of our comfort zones and place us in a place of faith. It is often challenging to build faith in regions of familiarity and unbelief. For that reason, Jesus had to move him from his home out of that city before he ministered to him.

Trust God Regardless

Sometimes, people are so weighed down by their unfavorable circumstances that it becomes difficult to walk by faith. But regardless of the adverse circumstances in your life, you can choose to put your faith in God. Your situation may be out of your control, but it is never out of God's control. Remember, broken things can become blessed when we allow God to do the mending. So, don't focus on what you can't do; instead, focus on what God can do.

Amazingly, God specializes in turning dead situations around. I am talking about situations that seem hopeless. We must choose to rely on His promises and believe Him against all odds. You have to choose to disregard the symptoms or the negative medical report to trust God for your healing. It's a matter of choice. And like I said earlier, you can't deny the diagnosis, but you can defy the verdict. There is a vast difference between the two. You live in a lie in denying the verdict, but in defying the verdict, you reaffirm the truth of God's word against every obvious fact of medicine.

Do Something Now!

And the way you demonstrate your faith is through your actions. You know, without faith, God has no business with you. But without action, your faith is dead—totally incapable of producing any result. The book of Hebrews talking about Noah said that he built the ark moved with fears of the impending flood, which was ultimately proof of his faith in the word of God. Never be found passive in your faith or taking actions that contradict your faith; that is a complete waste of time. Stop sitting on the sideline and watching things happen for other people, and step out in absolute faith to create your miracle! Step out and win!

CHAPTER NINE

Unwavering Faith

When challenges, negative circumstances, battles, or obstacles stare us in the face, only those with unwavering faith can stand. When things become so tough that even the strong are tempted to give up, you need to know where you stand. If you are faced with insurmountable challenges, you need an unshakable faith in God. Sincerely, it takes faith to face the issues of life. It takes faith to face negative medical diagnoses and beat the odds; it takes real Bible faith to accomplish impossible things.

Persistent, unstoppable, undefeatable, and unwavering faith—faith that does not wobble around with fear and unbelief is a rare treasure to possess, especially in difficult moments. The Bible talks about holding fast to our faith without wavering.

"Let us hold fast the profession of our faith without wavering; (for he is faithful that promised;)" (Hebrews 10:23 (KJV))

When it says we should not waver, it simply means that we will likely be surrounded by unpleasant circumstances that could cause us to waver. But through it all, we can have faith in God.

God is Ever Faithful

Faith is impossible without a faithful God, who can fulfill His every promise and is also trustworthy. We trust God only because He is trustworthy. He is dependable, reliable, and full of honor. His quality of honor is reflected in his integrity. The word "integrity" comes from the root word "integer," a mathematical term representing the number one. Integrity means one thing—with your word. And that, of course, is a perfect description of God.

"In the beginning was the Word, and the Word was with God, and the Word was God." (John 1:1 (KJV))

God is one with His word, which means that you cannot separate Him from His word. In other words, you can trust His word in the same way you trust Him. There will be times when it appears that what you are believing God for will never come true; there will be times when your best efforts will yield no positive results; however if you choose to hold on to your faith, you will eventually receive it.

Amazingly, His word can create what it says and become what it says. This is just amazing! So, when God makes a promise, He is faithful enough to fulfill it. In other words, you can take the "check" to the bank and cash it because it cannot fail. Remember, the book of Hebrew says, "he is faithful that promised..." (Hebrews 10:23 (KJV))

Without integrity (the faithfulness of God), faith is impossible. And without faith, life will be miserable. When the unexpected happens, when there is an unavoidable setback in your life, faith is the only weapon capable of initiating a turnaround. I am talking about unshakable and unwavering faith in God.

1. Faith is the ability to see things that don't exist.

One of the most outstanding qualities of faith is the capacity to see something that doesn't exist. When we say it does not exist, we mean that such things are not yet revealed to the physical senses. The truth is that from the moment you think about the possibility of something, it exists, but manifesting physically is a different thing altogether. Therefore, a person of faith can see things that others can't see long before they eventually show up physically.

"Faith is the substance of things hoped for, the evidence of things not seen." (Hebrew 11:1 (KJV))

Look at that, "faith is a substance" and "the evidence." If faith is a substance and evidence, then the first object of faith truly does exist, except it is not yet visible to the physical eyes. Therefore, genuine faith will act as if it is so—it will align with perceived spiritual evidence or assurance.

"While we look not at the things which are seen, but at

the things which are not seen: for the things which are seen are temporal; but the things which are not seen are eternal." (2 Corinthians 4:18 (KJV))

2. Faith is stepping out when you don't understand the whole.

Sincerely, only faith can take action on something not fully understood. Understand that the walk of faith is the walk of the Spirit. And like the Bible rightly said, "We walk by faith, not by sight" (2 Corinthians 5:7 (KJV)), meaning that our actions are not governed by what we see but by what we don't yet see. Most people of faith revealed in Scripture acted on their faith despite not understanding everything. You will probably be dead if you wait to understand everything before acting.

Look at Noah. He was instructed to build a ship (Noah's ark); even though he did not understand all God intended to do, he acted on God's instruction. Later in the book of Hebrews, we are told that it was a move of faith.

"By faith Noah, being warned of God of things not seen as yet, moved with fear, prepared an ark to the saving of his house; by the which he condemned the world, and became heir of the righteousness which is by faith." (Hebrews 11:7 (KJV))

For example, when God told Abraham to leave his parents and go to a totally strange land, he obeyed, not knowing or understanding exactly how things would play out. That is faith in action.

"By faith Abraham, when he was called to go out into a place which he should after receive for an inheritance, obeyed; and he went out, not knowing whither he went." (Hebrews 11:8 (KJV))

3. Faith is persisting even when you don't feel like it.

Faith is not a feeling; it is an internal conviction that compels you to act on the word of God. Faith, therefore, would persist even in times of difficulty when everything seems to contradict your belief. I am talking about times when you feel like giving up. Faith will move you to take steps forward regardless of how you feel. Life is full of challenges, and I mean real-time situations capable of driving someone crazy. Here is how Paul describes such moments:

"We are troubled on every side, yet not distressed; we are perplexed, but not in despair; Persecuted, but not forsaken; cast down, but not destroyed;" (2 Corinthians 4:8-9 (KJV))

When you face difficult times, you are tempted to go the way of your feelings, ignoring the substance of God's word. But then, it is in such moments that you need to demonstrate your unwavering faith by being persistent. For instance, when Abraham faced a difficult time, his faith did not waver. He did not allow his feelings or the pressure from his circumstances to get in the way of his faith. In fact, not only is it that he refused to consider the obvious dead state of his physical body, we are told that he refused to stagger at the promise of God.

"And being not weak in faith, he considered not his own body now dead, when he was about a hundred years old, neither yet the deadness of Sara's womb: He staggered not at the promise of God through unbelief; but was strong in faith, giving glory to God." (Romans 4:19-20 (KJV))

He was so persuaded of God's capacity to keep His promise that he did not let his feelings rob him of his miracle son—Isaac. You cannot afford to depend on your feelings. Instead, you are to persist until the end. Your feelings will fail you woefully, but your faith will stand the test of time. Your faith will produce its object with persistence. Unwavering faith is, therefore, a most invaluable asset in the race of life. The question is, how do you develop an unwavering faith like Abraham?

Four Ways to Develop Unwavering Faith

The following will help you in developing unwavering faith:

1. Accepting God's plan for your life.

One of the most assuring discoveries that any child of God can make is this: God has a plan for everyone of us. The prophet Jeremiah declared, "For I know the thoughts that I think toward you, saith the Lord, thoughts of peace, and not of evil, to give you an expected end." (Jeremiah 29:11 (KJV))

This is not an empty promise but a divine prerogative to take you somewhere designed by God. He is a God of purpose, plans, and objectivity; He never does anything for its fun. The very fact that you are here is proof that God created you for a specific purpose.

However, this purpose must be discovered and accepted by you before you can find fulfillment in it. Your purpose is not your creation but only your discovery. When you discover that plan, you are said to have a vision. A vision is, therefore, God's revelation to man. This revelation can come through an encounter, like in the case of Paul (Saul). When he encountered Jesus Christ on his way to Damascus, his purpose was revealed (Acts 26:16-19).

Based on such a clear vision for your life, unwavering faith is born inside of you. If you are sure that God has a definite plan for you and come to accept it absolutely, your faith will become rock-solid.

2. Be ready to risk failure.

To develop unwavering faith, you must be ready to risk failure. Faith in itself is risky. It was risky for Peter to step out of the boat's comfort, believing he would walk on water just like Jesus. Of course, when he shifted his gaze from Jesus, he began to sink. But it took the risk of faith to step out in the first place.

"And Peter answered him and said, Lord, if it is thou, bid me come unto thee on the water. And he said, Come. And when Peter was come down out of the ship, he walked on the water, to go to Jesus." (Mark 14:28-2 (KJV))

Good news! God promised to be there for us in any situation, no matter how risky.

"When thou passest through the waters, I will be with thee; and through the rivers, they shall not overflow thee: when thou walkest through the fire, thou shalt not be burned; neither shall the flame kindle upon thee." (Isaiah 43:2 (KJV))

"But Jesus beheld them, and said unto them, with men this is impossible, but with God all things are possible." (Matthew 19:26 (KJV))

3. Always expect the best.

Unwavering faith always expects the best of every situation. There are times when it would seem like what you are believing God for will never happen; there are times when your best effort will yield no positive result; yet if you choose to hold on to your faith, you will eventually get it. But you must have a positive expectation. It was by unwavering faith that Jericho's wall came down.

"By faith, the walls of Jericho fell down, after they were compassed about seven days." (Hebrews 11:30 (KJV))

Imagine you were the one instructed to match around the walls of Jericho for seven days. And out of obedience, you stepped out and started matching around the wall. But then, after six whole days, nothing seems to change. The wall is still standing, and the giants are still watching. Yet unwavering faith knows that what God promised will come to pass.

4. Never give up no matter what.

Unwavering faith never gives up, never quits, no matter what. In life, you are either a quitter or a winner. If you quit, you will lose, but you will emerge a winner if you choose to stick it out with God; if you refuse to quit. Many people quit because they are weary of waiting too long for their promises. If you want to operate in unwavering faith, you must deliberately refuse to quit. And just as the Bible declares, you will receive your promise.

"And let us not be weary in well doing: for in the due season, we shall reap if we faint not." (Galatians 6:9 (KJV))

Unwavering faith is absolute dependence on God. It is taking steps based on your confidence in God's promises. Abraham is called "the father of faith" because he had absolute faith and trust in the promises of God. This faith, trust, dependence, and confidence make extraordinary things happen. God blesses people who are not afraid to depend upon Him, trust him, and seek his guidance. Whatever you're manifesting in your life comes down to the degree of your faith. If you have unwavering faith, nothing will be impossible for you. You will see the realization of your dreams.

Chapter Ten

Choose Faith Over Fear

One of the greatest hindrances to the working of faith in many people's lives is fear. Fear keeps people from taking the necessary steps required to succeed in life. If you don't take the corresponding action, you will not be able to achieve your dreams, you will not be able to bring pleasure to God. If you allow yourself to be paralyzed by fear, you cannot please God as you should.

Fear will hinder your growth; it will hinder your faith and hinder you from being all you were created to be. If you are afraid, you will not say what you should say and do the things you should do, which means your potential and possibilities will be locked up forever. You cannot afford to let fear rob you of your God-given opportunities in life; you cannot allow fear to immobilize you from taking corresponding actions required to advance your destiny.

Joseph Campbell, an American Professor, says about fear: "The cave you fear to enter holds the treasure you seek." There is also this saying that "fear is false evidence appearing real." In other words, the majority of what many people fear are things that don't even exist. There are different reasons why many people are afraid. Many people have all kinds of fears; the fear of premature death, fear of unpaid debts, fear of failure, fear of success, fear of adversity, loss of a loved one, loss of job, fear of misfortune, etc. The painful fact is that many people don't even realize why they are afraid. Fear shows ignorance; every time you are afraid, you demonstrate your ignorance of something valuable.

The Choice is Yours

The capacity to make choices by ourselves is probably one of God's greatest gifts. Your choice empowers you to determine the course of your life. Your choice is your decision, and your decision determines your destiny or outcome. Now, for every choice you make, there are consequences. And while you have control over your choices, you do not have control over the consequences of your choices; the consequences are controlled by the laws that govern your choices. Amazingly, these are automatic. Indeed, the power of choice is truly a miracle from God, meaning that you can choose to live by faith or by fear. And in times of great uncertainty, such as we are experiencing now, one of the wisest decisions you will have to make is to choose faith over fear.

Your Boldness, Your Advantage

God knows the importance of getting fear out of your space. He knows the level of damage that fear can inflict on his children, and that is why the Scripture is full of the phrase, "fear not!". Some Bible scholars say it appears about 365 times in the Bible. That is like one for each day. In Paul's epistle to the book of Philippians, he admonished believers never to fear.

"And in nothing terrified by your adversaries: which is to them an evident token of perdition, but to you of salvation, and that of God." (Philippians 1:28 (KJV))

Here is how it is rendered in the New Living Translation:

"Don't be intimidated by your enemies. This will be a sign to them that they are going to be destroyed, but that you are going to be saved, even by God himself." (Philippians 1:28 (NLT))

If you allow yourself to be intimidated by your enemies or fear of whatever else you may be dealing with, you will be defeated. Most people are first defeated by fear before circumstances defeat them. But if you face your fears and dare to persist, you will conquer them. As a Christian, you must refuse to be intimidated by fear; refuse to allow fear to rob you of your inheritance in God. God wants us to be bold, no matter what we confront. And to manifest that kind of boldness, understand you have been given the spirit of boldness, not fear.

"For God hath not given us the spirit of fear, but of power, and of love, and of a sound mind." (2 Timothy 1:7 (KJV))

Know Who You Are

Why are you so scared? I mentioned earlier that many

people fear, and the basic reason is ignorance. For instance, if you don't know who you are, whose you are, what you have, and what you can do; fear will creep in; on the other hand, if you have revealed knowledge of who you are (in God), boldness will naturally erupt from your inside. I mean, even amid the most challenging circumstances. That means you will remain calm because of what you know. The Bible says the people that do know their God shall be strong and do exploits (Daniel 11:32).

The prophet Elisha and his servant were surrounded by soldiers who came to arrest him, but Elisha continued as though nothing was at stake. His servant was terrified, wondering why Elisha was so calm amid an obvious threat to his life. Of course, Elisha saw the apprehension in the young man's eyes and decided to help him. So, he prayed that God would open his servant's eyes to see those who were for them.

"And when the servant of the man of God was risen early, and gone forth, behold, a host compassed the city both with horses and chariots. And his servant said unto him, Alas, my master! What shall we do? And he answered, Fear not: for they that be with us are more than they that be with them. And Elisha prayed and said, Lord, I pray thee, open his eyes, that he may see. And the Lord opened the eyes of the young man; and he saw: and, behold, the mountain was full of horses and chariots of fire round about Elisha." (2 Kings 6:15-17 (KJV))

Apparently, those angels had been there, but Elisha's servant did not see them. As a result, he was apprehensive. If you are ignorant of who you are and what is available at your disposal, you will become afraid. I pray for you sincerely from my heart. May every fear disappear from you today!

Jesus Knew Who He Was

One of the greatest revelations that will change your life is discovering who you are in Christ. If you discover who God has made you, to be you will conquer fear forever. This was one secret Jesus had that gave him an edge over the circumstances of life. Jesus knew exactly who he was. He knew that demons should bow. And because of that, He was not intimidated by any circumstance, problem, or even Herod. He was not intimidated or scared by the betrayal of Judas or by death. He knew they were fulfilling their roles based on His heavenly father's power given to them. He knew that everything would work in his favor because He was the son of God. So, if you discover who you are, fear will die a natural death.

Renew Your Mind

The world system wants to control all of us. It wants to control how we think, feel and act. It wants to control our language. Today, every aspect of our communication has been infiltrated by the language of fear. So, you hear people say things like, "I am afraid it might rain." "I am afraid I can't make it." "I am afraid it won't work." Why not just say, "I think it might rain, or I am sorry, I might not make it to the office today. And the problem is that many believers have given so much attention to circular media that their entire mindset has been completely hijacked. So, they think about fear, talk about fear, and act fear.

Sometimes you hear believers say something; and wonder whether they are born again. How could a child of God say, "I was scared to death."? How could you talk like that? Well, it could be that you have never really been exposed to the word of God. But if you continue to talk like that, I bet you will get yourself into serious trouble.

The good news is that you can recover yourself from such satanically controlled vocabulary. If you want to recover yourself, you need to start renewing your mind with the word. Your life is transformed to the level that you accept the responsibility to renew your mind with the word of God.

"And be not conformed to this world: but be ye transformed by the renewing of your mind, that ye may prove what that good is, and acceptable, and perfect, will of God." (Roman 12:2 (KJV))

But someone may say, "but things are rough for me right now. I am only stating the fact. How could I deny the facts?" Well, I am not saying you should deny the facts; all I am saying is that you can overcome whatever situation you are dealing with. Regardless of what you may be going through, you can choose to walk in faith instead of fear.

Feed Your Faith, Starve Your Fear

Fear and faith cannot co-exist. Once fears take over, faith disappears. Fear is just the opposite of faith. Both faith and fear operate by the same law, the law of hearing. When you open your ears to the word of God, it will enter your heart and automatically birth faith. The Bible tells us in the book of Romans that faith comes from hearing the word (Romans 10:17).

In the same vein, fear comes from hearing—giving your ear to the wrong information. This is one of the deadliest side-effects of spending time with circular media. Most circular media platforms promote more negatives than positives. So, giving your ears to them will be like arming your enemies against yourself. You cannot play around at 10 degrees and wonder why you caught the flu. In the same way, you cannot feed your mind on all the harmful, faith-draining, fear-promoting contents of the present and expect to still walk in faith. It just doesn't work that way.

But if you want faith to take over your heart, if you're going to get rid of fear, you have to feed your faith and starve your fears. Choose faith over fear by investing quality time listening to and watching the right stuff. It is only as you control your thoughts that you can curb the activities of fear in your life.

Close the Door to Fear

Fear is like a forerunner to Satan. If you allow fear into your life, you will open the door to darkness, sickness, misfortune, losses, and satanic attacks. If you study the life of Job, you will notice that one of the things that opened him up to all kinds of crazy satanic attacks was his constant fear.

"For my sighing cometh before I eat, and my roarings are poured out like the waters. For the thing which I greatly feared is come upon me, and that which I was afraid of is come unto me. I was not in safety, neither had I rest, neither was I quiet, yet trouble came." (Job 3:24-26 (KJV))

The above Scripture gives us a clue why Job had to go through some of the most horrendous experiences of his life. He went through such times that if it were not for his perseverance and the help of God, he would have been completely wiped out. But he said it was fear that opened the door in the first place. Of course, we are aware of the conversation between God and Satan, yet it is clear that fear played a significant role. Once you get rid of fear, you have closed the door to every form of negativity. But it all begins with the decision to choose faith over fear.

About the Author

Harris McFarlane is the President of Dimension Financial Services. Also, the founder of Dimension Abundant Life Ministries, Rocky Hill, CT.

Harris is the author of *Claim the Promises of God and Prepare for a Miracle, and Focus on Purpose, Not Fear.* He and his wife, Jennifer, live in Connecticut with their daughter Nicole.

You can visit his website at www.dimensionministries.org and www.dimension-financial.com

www.ingramcontent.com/pod-product-compliance
Lightning Source LLC
Chambersburg PA
CBHW052114110526
44592CB00013B/1611

THE UNWAVERING FAITH

Faith is one of the believer's potent powers in the Bible. *The Unwavering Faith* attests to your absolute trust in God and His promises for your life. Abraham demonstrated this, "He did not waver at the promise of God through unbelief, but was strengthened in faith, giving glory to God" (Romans 4:20). This gave birth to an undeniable miracle in his life.

When the tide changes against you; and the floods of negativity seem to close in on your dreams, faith is your best bait to stay afloat. "By faith he forsook Egypt, not fearing the wrath of the King: for he endured, as seeing him who is invisible" (Hebrew 11:27). Faith is in the invisible. Faith is an attitude of mind. Moses had every reason to be afraid of going up against Pharaoh who was considered the most powerful man in the world. However, Moses knew he was responding to the highest authority.

The main goal of this book is to unlock this ultimate power of faith in you, thereby giving you wings to soar into new dimensions of accomplishment.

Rev. Harris D. McFarlane is the President of Dimension Financial Services. Also, the founder of Dimension Abundant Life Ministries, Rocky Hill, CT. Harris is the author of Claim the Promises of God, Prepare for a Miracle and Focus on Purpose, Not Fear.

He and his wife, Jennifer, live in Connecticut with their daughter Nicole. You can visit his website at www.dimensionministries.org and www.dimension-financial.com

ISBN 978-1-952098-97-0

I Found Love

My Journey of Hope, Perseverance, and Finding True Love

VERONICA BORNN